Same But Different Math

Same But Different Math is a powerful routine to help students improve their mathematical reasoning, clarify concepts and make critical connections between ideas. Popular math consultant Sue Looney takes you step-by-step through implementation so you can easily add this routine into your toolbox. She establishes the rationale for the routine and then walks you through specific examples of when to use it, how to use it and how to make specific connections for learners. Throughout the book, you'll find examples of lessons with images from a range of grade levels and mathematical content to show you the routine in action. There are also exercises for you to complete while reading to help you apply what you've learned, as well as a handy planning section with a template and resource links. In addition, there are Appendices featuring additional examples, which you can download from our website www.routledge.com/9781032126555 for classroom use. With the helpful features in this book, you'll come away confidently able to implement this routine, bringing all your students to deeper levels of understanding in math.

Dr. Sue Looney is a former elementary teacher who now provides professional development to PreK–12 educators across the country through Looney Consulting. She is dedicated to uncovering how children best learn mathematics. Follow her on Twitter @LooneyMath and visit her website www.looneymathconsulting.com.

T0383444

Same But Different Math

Helping Students Connect Concepts,
Build Number Sense, and
Deepen Understanding

Sue Looney

Routledge
Taylor & Francis Group

NEW YORK AND LONDON

Cover image: © Getty Images

First published 2023
by Routledge
605 Third Avenue, New York, NY 10158

and by Routledge
4 Park Square, Milton Park, Abingdon, Oxon, OX14 4RN

Routledge is an imprint of the Taylor & Francis Group, an informa business

Library of Congress Cataloging-in-Publication Data
A catalog record for this book has been requested

ISBN: 978-1-032-13204-4 (hbk)
ISBN: 978-1-032-12655-5 (pbk)
ISBN: 978-1-003-22813-4 (ebk)

DOI: 10.4324/9781003228134

Typeset in Palatino
by Apex CoVantage, LLC

Access the Support Material: www.routledge.com/9781032126555

Dedication

This book is dedicated to my partner in life, Dave Looney, who has continually believed in me. Special acknowledgment to Jess Looney for her creative genius, to Joey Looney for leading me to this routine and chasing his dreams, to Alyson Eaglen for believing in the power of *Same But Different Math* and providing images for the book and to my family and friends who inspire and lift me up daily.

Contents

Meet the Author   *viii*

Support Material   *ix*

Introduction   1

1 Why Use the *Same But Different Math* Routine?   6

2 When Should I Use This Routine?   14

3 A Routine With Students at the Center:
Part 1 of the Protocol   29

4 Teacher Moves: Part 2 of the Protocol   34

5 Now It's Your Turn!   40

References   47
Appendix A: Poem   49
Appendix B: Additional Images   50

Meet the Author

As a new teacher, Sue Looney became fascinated with teaching mathematics and began her journey to understand how children learn mathematics best. Inspired by the work of author Jonathon Kozol (*Savage Inequalities*, 1991), she became particularly interested in our most vulnerable and underrepresented populations and supporting the teachers that day in and day out serve these students with compassion, enthusiasm and kindness.

This learning journey has taken Sue to amazing places: from the elementary classroom to writing materials for preschool students to obtaining her doctorate and teaching preservice teachers at Boston University to speaking at conferences from coast to coast in the United States to writing two children's books and to volunteering in the Galapagos Islands. She has been fortunate for these experiences and to have met incredible educators along the way who have been willing to teach and inspire her. She is still curious, is still learning and has a deep respect for all educators.

Support Material

The Appendices of this book are also available online so you can easily print the pages for classroom use. To access them, go to the book product page at www.routledge.com/9781032126555 and click on Support Material.

Introduction

Same But Different Math is a powerful routine for use in math classrooms. In this book you will learn why this is true and how you can expertly use this routine anytime with your students to develop deep connectivity between mathematical ideas.

It has been many years since I learned about _Same But Different Math_, and I continue to be amazed by the power of these simple words. I have used this routine with learners from 2 years old through high school. The conversations that ensue are impactful, with long-reaching effects on understanding. I hope you are excited to learn with me. I invite you to take a journey with me to see how this routine can dramatically change your math instruction.

Let's begin by trying out the routine. I like to start with this example from early childhood even when I introduce this routine to older students. After all, what could be better than combining cuteness and math?

Take a look at the two images in Figure 0.1. What do you notice? What features are you drawn to? Think and reflect on the words and the language that come to mind.

Figure 0.1

DOI: 10.4324/9781003228134-1

What do you notice?

_____
_____
_____
_____
_____

Now, let's compare the two images. How are the two images the same? List all the things you see that are the same.

How are the two images the same?

_____
_____
_____
_____
_____

You might have said they are both dogs. They both are cute. They both have fur. They both show two dogs.

Next, how are the two images different? List all the ways in which they are different.

How are the two images different?

_____
_____
_____
_____
_____

You might have said the color of their fur is different. They are different kinds of dogs. They are different sizes. In one picture, they are wearing a bandana, and in the other, they are not.

While the two pictures are of different-looking dogs, they both show TWO dogs. You can see *two* in different ways. The mathematical feature we notice here is all about understanding two. The images are the same but different – they are the same in that they both show two dogs, but they are different because things such as the kind of dogs in the images are different.

Imagine if you were 4 years old, just learning about quantity and making sense of counting and numbers. This experience would have helped you build your understanding of what *two* means. By using this routine, you would have created a lasting connection to this concept.

Same But Different Math can be thought of as the exercise of compare and contrast, which many are familiar with from language arts activities or other domains. Using a mathematical lens to unpack this routine further, you can also think about *Same But Different Math* as an exercise in understanding equivalence. Here's an example of what I mean.

Let's try another! Take a moment to study the image in Figure 0.2. What do you notice? What is the same? What is different?

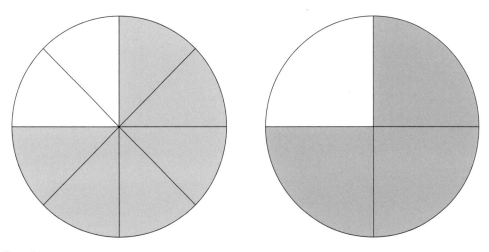

Figure 0.2

What is the same but different about the two fraction pictures?

You might have said they are the same because they are both circles, they are both broken up into pieces and they both have the same amount of area colored in. You might have said they are different because they are different colors and they have a different number of pieces colored in. Some of you might have gotten more specific and said they are different because one shows 6/8 and the other shows 3/4, but they are the same because those two fractions are equivalent. What happens here is that the image is used to open a discussion about a specific mathematical idea in a manner that allows students to construct those connections among and between ideas. When a discussion takes place grounded in student understanding, the class comes to a conclusion based on everyone's input. Important ideas are discussed collaboratively. Mathematical language is introduced. Student voice drives these discussions.

We profoundly impact mathematical reasoning with the routine
***Same But Different Math* when we help students clarify concepts
and make critical connections between ideas.**

Using this explicit language with students (How are these the same but different?) provides an opportunity for a deep impact on student learning. *Same But Different Math* is a routine that helps students build a network of ideas and is an approach to how they learn and think about all mathematics. You can embrace this approach and bring this powerful routine to all learners.

This book was created to empower you with all the tools you need to use this routine with your students. The chapters that follow provide the research behind the routine and answer the following questions:

◆ How did I learn about this routine? Why should you use this routine? What does the research tell us?
◆ When is the best time to use *Same But Different Math*?
◆ How exactly do you use this routine? What are the protocols and step-by-step actions can you take?
◆ How do you summarize an activity, and why is that important?
◆ Where can you find resources?
◆ How do you begin?

The book includes examples of lessons and images from a range of grade levels and mathematical content to help create a clear image of the routine in action. Chapters also contain exercises for you to complete while reading to get you engaged and apply what you learn in each chapter. The final chapter includes resource links and a planning activity to be sure you are ready to take action on all that you will have learned.

So grab a notebook. Grab a pencil. Find a cozy spot to read. And enjoy!

1

Why Use the *Same But Different Math* Routine?

Figure 1.1

I'd like to make the case with a story. It was 2005, and my son was 4 years old (Figure 1.1). His world was very black-and-white. New experiences and new language acquisition were challenges for him. He preferred to stick with what he knew and, as a result, was experiencing a lot of anxiety when outside his comfort zone. He was acting out in many ways, and life was becoming a struggle.

DOI: 10.4324/9781003228134-2

What we came to understand in working with speech-and-language pathology quite literally changed everything. We learned that our son was having trouble sorting any new information coming his way. He was not making connections between ideas, and therefore, each new experience was disconnected for him. He could not see overlap and had not developed categorical thinking. He was attempting to sort his world into so many different categories that he was easily overwhelmed. What he needed was support in developing a more connected view of the world.

Helping our son make sense of language, new information and his environment dramatically changed his behavior, lowering his anxiety and opening him up to a whole new way of experiencing things. When we understood how his brain worked, we learned to ask just the right question, shifting his thinking and changing his trajectory as a learner. It turns out that the *just-right* question we learned to ask was, **"What is the same but different?"**

This question became the norm in our household, always pointing out how things were the same but different. Here is a typical example. "We are at the beach. You know all about beaches. There's sand and water. We swim. But THIS beach is different. There's a dock we could swim out to." We were calling our son's attention to the common features of things, making things comfortable while helping him form a connection to something new. The amazing thing was that through using this language explicitly and practicing this repeatedly, he began to do the same. He began to attend to categorical thinking and the features of things and learned to make links and connections. His world became less black-and-white. We are forever grateful for the speech-and-language pathologist who led us to a deeper understanding of how our son made sense of his world. To this day, the power of these words amazes me. *Same But Different* are three powerful little words.

Grayscale Thinking and the Power of BUT

The activity of *Same But Different Math* is an activity where two things are *compared and contrasted*, calling attention to both how they are the same and how they are different. When we consider the research behind how children learn and make sense of their surroundings, we can better understand the inherent power in this activity as it connects to the development of grayscale thinking. Understanding this routine from the point of view of speech-and-language pathology allows you to profoundly impact mathematical reasoning with the routine of *Same But Different Math*.

So what exactly is grayscale thinking? Grayscale thinking is the ability to see the world as having some middle ground versus being a world of black-and-white. For example, there is something between happy and sad, between short and long and so on. People who have trouble with grayscale thinking tend to be rigid and get stressed when life doesn't fall into one category or another. "The problem with black and white thinking is that it usually does battle in a world that is nuanced and gray," says Byron Williams (2006) in his article on the subject. The routine of *Same But Different Math* helps call attention to the features of things – and how we can connect something new to something we are already familiar with, helping develop flexible grayscale thinking.

Have you noticed that the routine is called Same BUT Different, not Same AND Different or Same OR Different? Let's tackle the idea of why we don't say OR, why we don't ask students to decide and defend if images are the same or if they are different. This either–or thinking forces students to continue to sort their world into black-and-white. It's either this OR that. The power of *Same But Different Math* lies in doing the exact opposite of that— exploring the intersection. Using the word BUT, we juxtapose ideas and hint at the thought that the ideas move beyond similarities. Yes, something is the same about the two ideas presented, BUT there are also differences. There is more to the story. Students are not asked to choose one or the other; rather, a discussion is framed about playing with ideas in the space of overlap, grayscale thinking, sorting and connecting ideas.

All roads always lead back to math (Figure 1.2).

Figure 1.2

One of the reasons students struggle in math is that they fail to make connections. For some children (those lacking grayscale thinking), every concept they learn is its own entity without any connection to the larger network of mathematical ideas. Just like the young child who struggles to see the connections between information from their surroundings, someone who you might say has "poorly developed number sense" might actually see each number as its own entity and not part of the larger number system.

Ask a young child where they can find 8 on a number line to 10. If they don't race toward the end of that number line, knowing that 8 is near 10, but instead start at the number one and make their way up the number line, that *could* be an indication that they are lacking a systematic understanding of the counting system. They can only locate 8, for example, by considering each consecutive number starting at 1. A mathematical conversation using the language of same but different that calls attention to how a new concept in math is the same as a familiar and comfortable concept but different in a specific way, helps children grow a network of connected ideas. This reduces anxiety as children become the sense-makers in the conversation. If we keep going with this number line example, I can ask a child, "How are 1 and 8 the same but different?" I can show them both images on the number line to be compared, like in Figure 1.3.

Figure 1.3

Take a moment to answer the following questions and notice how this helps you build a connection between the numbers 1, 8 and all the numbers on the number line showing 1 through 10.

How are the two images the same?

_____

_____

_____

_____

_____

How are the two images different?

_____
_____
_____
_____
_____

By calling children's attention to each new concept and how it is the same in some way as something they already know, but different in a key way, we help them grow their network of connections and develop a robust understanding of concepts. A mathematical conversation using the language of same but different that calls attention to how a new concept in math is the same as that other familiar and comfortable concept but different in a specific way is a tremendously useful conversation in growing that network of connections.

When using the *Same But Different Math* routine students consider the features, the characteristics, the defining qualities of what they are comparing. They notice the overlap of ideas as well as unique distinguishing qualities. When we begin by specifically saying, "These two things are the same," we lower cognitive tension. This is the beginning of building a bridge to understanding.

Another good example of the power of *Same But Different Math* to build bridges to understanding comes from the topic of place value. Place-value understanding requires an integration of new and difficult-to-construct concepts of grouping by tens (the base-ten concept) with procedural knowledge of how groups are recorded in our place-value scheme, how numbers are written and how they are spoken (Van De Walle, Teaching Developmentally, 2013). Children are introduced to a new unit called a ten that is simultaneously two things – one ten and ten ones. One ten is the same value as ten ones, but it is different in that it is one ten. Accepting that something can be two same-but-different ideas simultaneously is quite complex. Using the image in Figure 1.4 and facilitating a conversation about what is the same but different helps students make sense of this complex idea.

After allowing students to think and turn and talk about Figure 1.4, the following conversation can take place.

Figure 1.4

Teacher:	Who would like to tell me how these two images are the same but different?
Eneya:	Both pictures show ten cubes.
Teacher:	Can you come up and show us?
Eneya:	(using a pointer). This one here has ten cubes all stuck together. See? 1, 2, 3, 4, 5, 6, 7, 8, 9, 10. And this one here, there are 10, but they are not stuck together.
Teacher:	Should we count those, too?
Eneya:	1, 2, 3, 4, 5 and 6, 7, 8, 9, 10.
Teacher:	Can someone else put in your own words what Eneya just said?
Ryan:	Eneya said they both show 10, but in one picture, they are stuck together, and in the other, they are not.
Teacher:	Does everyone agree that both pictures show 10 cubes, but they look different?
Class responds:	Yes!
Teacher:	So we can have 10 cubes shown in different ways. But either way, we still have 10 cubes?

Using this explicit language with students (How are these the same but different?), we have an opportunity for a deep impact on student learning. We are teaching a way of thinking: grayscale thinking, categorical thinking, building not only a network of ideas but also an approach to how we learn and think about all of mathematics.

Let's dig into the research a little bit more.

Exploring Executive Functioning: What is Executive Functioning and What Does It Have to Do With Same But Different?

According to the Harvard University Center for the Developing Child, "[e]xecutive function and self-regulation skills are the mental processes that enable us to plan, focus attention, remember instructions, and juggle multiple tasks successfully." You might think about executive functioning in light of what an executive of a company does. An executive needs to be organized, self-motivated and strategic. They need to have the ability to evaluate a situation, create a solution and act on it. An executive must be capable of using prior learning to predict outcomes and to react and approach problem-solving situations flexibly (Meltzer, 2007).

These skills come into play in many aspects of life but, in particular, in mathematics with the connection to problem-solving and mental flexibility. These skills are developing over time and are directly related to the experiences that a child has as they grow and develop. We can enhance a child's mental flexibility by intentionally creating opportunities for students to tap into these skills. *Same But Different Math* is one such way to do this. We build mental flexibility in how students make sense of math concepts as a connected set of ideas in which two things can be both the same and different simultaneously.

Compare and Contrast Repurposed for the Math Classroom

The routine of *Same But Different Math* takes the well-known task of compare and contrast, which is typically applied within language or history classrooms, and reframes it around a mathematical conversation.

According to research by Marzano, Pickering and Pollock (2010), when students are asked to compare and contrast, they gain significantly in achievement. In fact, in their study, they found that students gained 45 percentile points on average.

Looking more deeply at why compare and contrast is so powerful, Silver breaks the strengths down as the following:

- ◆ Strengthen student memories
- ◆ Develop higher-order thinking skills
- ◆ Increase student comprehension
- ◆ Enhance students' writing in the content areas
- ◆ Develop students' habits of mind

(Silver, 2010)

Each of these strengths is important in the context of a math learner. Of course, we want to encourage strong memories, higher-order thinking and comprehension. How would enhancing writing help in a math classroom? When we ask our students to put thoughts into writing, the skills are multi-layered. Having students speak and then write about how concepts are the same but different affords them the opportunity to formulate, articulate and solidify their thoughts. In essence, this is an opportunity to concretize their thinking.

And, perhaps the most exciting strength, is the power to develop a habit of mind. Assimilating new information into preexisting information using a compare-and-contrast process with the *Same But Different Math* routine helps students make sense of their world. With practice and over time, learners internalize this as a process for acquiring knowledge. As teachers, we provide students the opportunity to practice this skill in the form of a lesson. When this becomes a habit of mind, it is simply how a child views sensemaking and learning.

Now that you understand why *Same But Different Math* is powerful, how it is grounded in research and how it is designed to impact student learning, you can begin to learn when and how to use this routine. In the next chapter, we unpack *when* it is most optimal to use this routine.

2

When Should I Use This Routine?

You have already learned why *Same But Different Math* is a powerful routine, but when is it best to use this routine? How will you be prepared to use this question effectively at those "just right" moments in instruction?

It is recognized that in the classroom too much is happening for teachers to make new decisions in response to every circumstance. . . . Nevertheless, the very complexity that makes routines necessary also requires teachers to be making and remaking decisions in response to circumstances pressing in the classroom. This key teaching role – that of decision maker – is sometimes not fully acknowledged in teacher development programs and even by teachers themselves.

(Mousley, 2001)

A student's opportunity to learn is directly related to these decisions their teacher makes. Teachers are receiving information from their students constantly, leading to on-the-spot decisions of what to do next. I call this feedback loop the Teaching for Number Sense Cycle (Figure 2.1).

During a math lesson teachers work in a cycle of understanding, building and growing students' number sense. Instead of being in a "turn-the-page mode," where the next page of the textbook or the next task is what happens, powerful teaching means operating in an understanding mode. And that looks like the Teaching for Number Sense Cycle.

DOI: 10.4324/9781003228134-3

Teaching for Number Sense Cycle

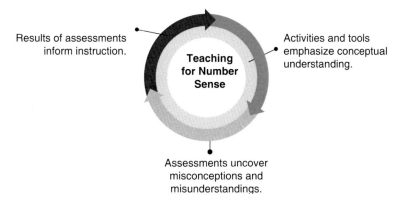

Results of assessments inform instruction.

Teaching for Number Sense

Activities and tools emphasize conceptual understanding.

Assessments uncover misconceptions and misunderstandings.

Figure 2.1

Breaking Down the Teaching for Number Sense Cycle

Step 1: Activities and Tools Emphasize Conceptual Understanding

When preparing for instruction, you consider what it is you hope students will understand as a result of their lesson—not what you will *do* but rather what you hope they will understand. This is an important distinction. Activities and materials are selected to build that conceptual understanding.

Step 2: Assessments Uncover Naïve Conceptions and Misunderstandings

From there, you become curious and notice how students are doing. This type of assessment can be both formal and informal. Educators are constantly taking in information like a detective. What do you see? What does this student understand? What evidence do you have of their understanding? At this step, teachers can complete this sentence: I see that the student is _____. This gathering of information allows the next step in decision-making to match a student's journey toward conceptual understanding.

Step 3: Results of Assessments Inform Instruction

Based on that assessment information, you decide the next step. Because I see _____, the best next step is _____. Herein lies the opportunity for powerful instruction. What you decide to do next impacts a student's opportunity to learn. It is when you get curious about what you see and learn from your students that this cycle leads to deep learning.

And, then, the cycle of teaching and learning goes around and around.

What does all this have to do with the *Same But Different Math* number sense routine? *Same But Different Math* comes in as a routine that can be used in response to the feedback loop. By asking the question how things are the same but different, students are encouraged to construct their own conceptual understanding, solidifying their understanding.

My goal with this book is to empower you as the decision-maker in the classroom to use the routine of *Same But Different Math* at the most opportune moments. I want you to be prepared to confidently use this routine at the exact just right moments as they present themselves during your instruction.

There are three distinct times where you can decide to use the *Same But Different Math* routine to maximize impact on student learning:

◆ Connecting concepts
◆ Naive conceptions
◆ Concepts learned in pairs

Connecting Concepts

Mathematics is a series of connected and interrelated conceptual ideas. As math educators, we strive to teach students to connect and make sense of a network of ideas. Each *new* idea builds on a *previous* idea in some way. By explicitly building those connections, students are better equipped to make sense of new concepts and access that information in meaningful ways. Think of this as the process of building bridges.

Let's unpack some examples.

Early Childhood – Counting

When students are learning to count, they connect the idea that the next number stated is the same as adding one more. If I ask what is one more than 5 or if I ask what number comes after 5, the answer is 6. It's the same. This may seem very obvious to you, but to a new learner, this is a big leap in making sense of the counting sequence. Knowing that the next number in the sequence is connected to the quantitative meaning of the number is an important milestone.

If you are working on the concept of "one more than," this is a perfect opportunity to provide students an explicit opportunity to make that connection. Let's look at how *Same But Different Math* builds a bridge between these two ideas in a kindergarten classroom.

Figure 2.2

At first glance, the two images in Figure 2.2 look very different. Students usually all notice that one image shows numbers and the other image shows cubes, as you can see on the blue and green sticky notes. One student might count all the cubes and share that one side shows 11 and the other side shows 6. The teacher can then introduce the idea that they could also be the same by saying, "In what ways are the two images the same but different? Can you now find ways in which they are the same?" She can then ask students to think silently for one minute and then turn and talk with a partner.

Study the image in Figure 2.3 for a moment. Notice what happened with the students who were prompted with the question, "How are they the same but different?"

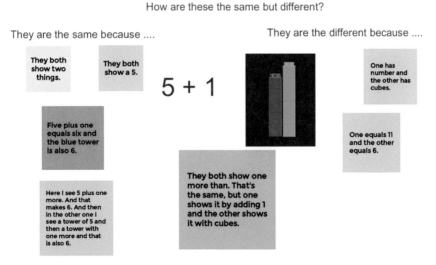

Figure 2.3

After allowing for both think time and partner talk, the teacher pulls the class back together, and you can see the shift in the discussion. The mathematical conversation moved from counting and adding to the realm of connections and ultimately to generalization. The orange sticky note shows the conclusion the class came to: "They both show one more than. That's the same, but one shows it by adding 1, and the other shows it with cubes." This is very big thinking for kindergarten students who are engaged with making sense of a connection among counting numbers, quantity and addition. *Same But Different Math* provides a forum to move students to deeper levels of understanding.

Intermediate Grades

What are some other concepts that connect? Let's look at an example from third grade. The foundation of understanding multiplication is the connection to repeated addition. Students who are working in an additive phase of understanding can make sense of $4 + 4 + 4$ as such

$$4 + 4 = 8$$
$$8 + 4 = 12$$
Therefore, $4 + 4 + 4 = 12$.

When students make sense of multiplication, they realize that 3×4 means three groups of 4. As they learn their multiplication facts, they move from an additive solution pathway to a multiplicative solution where they see 3 and 4 as factors with a product of 12. Using an array for multiplication helps students connect repeated addition to multiplication. Because repeated addition and multiplication ARE the same but different.

In this third-grade classroom, the teacher asks the students what is the same but different. She gives them one minute of silent think time, and then they move into partners to discuss. Take a moment to notice the feedback gathered during the whole-class share as seen in Figures 2.4 and 2.5.

At first, the students notice color and shape, saying, "They both have the same color dots," and "Both have dots in boxes." These are easy entry points to the conversation as they compare and contrast the images. As students are given time and ideas are shared collectively, as you read about in the previous example, the conversation shifts. Students begin to attend to the deeper mathematics. Both images show 20, but they arrange 20 differently. The image on the right that shows 4 columns of 5 dots lends itself to repeated addition (or even counting) whereas the rectangle image on the left lends

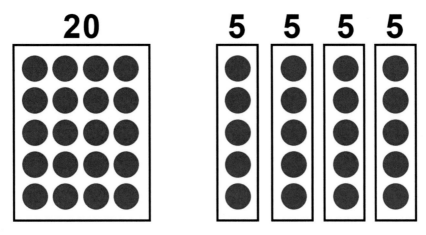

Figure 2.4

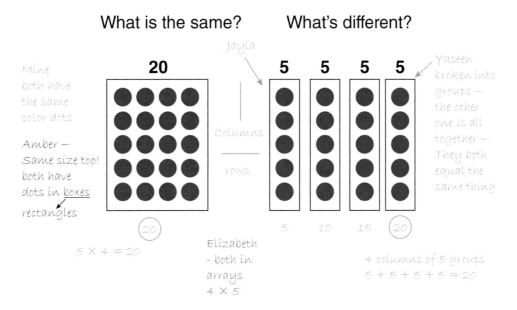

Figure 2.5

itself to seeing multiplication as an array. Ultimately, the solution is the same, but how we arrange equal groups impacts the matching equation we might write and how we think about a solution path. Interesting. This third grade left the conversation deeply thinking about the connection between addition and multiplication, which will now propel them forward in their mathematical journey toward understanding.

It is here, within this interconnected web of mathematical ideas that we can find the beauty in mathematics. Math is playful, creative and yet purposeful and precise. As you work through your curriculum goals and concepts, learn to be mindful of those connections. And as you encounter them, ask your students to play in this space and make sense of the growing set of complex ideas by asking them what is the same but different.

> **Consider the topics that you teach. List concepts that connect. What images, numbers or words might you use in creating a same-but-different task for your students?**
>
> _____
> _____
> _____
> _____
> _____

Naive Conceptions

When learning mathematics, there are common misconceptions that students make. Or we might instead call these early or naive conceptions.

> *The term "misconception" implies incorrectness or error due to the prefix "mis." From a child's perspective, their idea is a reasonable and viable conception based on their experiences in different contexts or in their daily life activities. When children's conceptions are deemed to be in conflict with the accepted meanings in mathematics, the term misconceptions has tended to be used. Therefore some researchers or educators prefer to use the term "alternative conception" instead of "misconception." Other terms sometimes used for misconceptions or terms related to misconceptions include students' mental models, children's arithmetic, preconceptions, naïve theories, conceptual primitives, private concepts, alternative frameworks, and critical barriers.*
>
> (Fujii, 2014)

I like how this language flips our thought process as teachers into a strength-based frame of mind.

During instruction, you might notice that many students are thinking about a concept the same way, and you'd like to move them forward in their understanding. Your in-the-moment decision of how to respond to what you are seeing can be to use the routine of *Same But Different Math*. Here's an example.

Early Childhood

When learning to count, many students have trouble learning to read, write and make sense of teen numbers. It is common for a student learning fourteen to write that is 41. This happens because they first hear four and, therefore, decide it makes sense to write the four first. In the English language, however, we don't do that. We make the teen numbers complicated and sort of speak them in the reverse of how we write them. This is a good opportunity to unpack what is happening here. Playing around in the gray space of mathematics, looking for the connection – or lack of in this case – between the spoken and the written words (Figure 2.6) – is an opportunity for sensemaking. Rather than stating a rule to children, posing the question, "How are these numbers the same but different?" allows them to notice and respond.

14   41

Figure 2.6

Here's how students responded to this *Same But Different Math* image.

Mrs. Valdés: Take a moment and look at the numbers I've written on the board. Think about what you are seeing with this question in mind. How are they the same but different? How are the two numbers different? Answer using these sentence frames: They are the same because _____. They are different because _____.

  After one minute of silent think time, Mrs. Valdés has the students turn and talk and then brings the class back together to share their thoughts.

Take a moment to notice the feedback gathered during the whole-class share as seen in Figure 2.7.

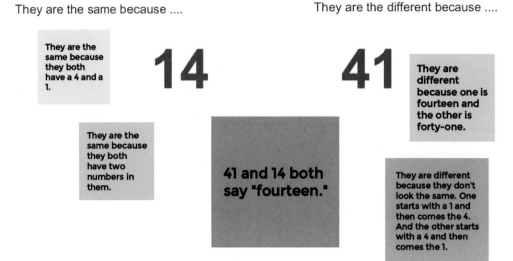

Figure 2.7

The conversation starts out with visual statements. The students *see* the numerals 1 and 4 in both 14 and 41. They notice, however, that they are in a different order. And then Mrs. Valdés receives the pink comment. Here is a naive conception – both of those numbers are spoken as fourteen. Mrs. Valdés has noticed previously that other students have this idea based on a lesson on teen numbers. She knows and anticipates that this will cause tension and meaningful conversation. She harnesses the power of *Same But Different Math* as a vehicle to allow students to wrestle with this. Here's the conversation that followed.

Mrs. Valdés:	That's very interesting. So whether I write 14 or 41 either one I read as 14. Who agrees?
	Many students start signaling, "Yes, that's the case."
Mrs. Valdés:	How would I write the number 41? Turn and talk to your partner and then please write 41 on your whiteboards.
	The students all hold up a whiteboard with 41 written on it.
Mrs. Valdés:	We all agree that forty-one is written as 41. Some of us also think that I read 41 as fourteen. Can a written number be read two different ways?

About half the students signal, "Yes, that's an OK thing to happen." Some are now deeply confused as is evident right away with loud exclamations like "Huh?"

And a couple of students are just about to explode with their disagreement.

Rather than call on those students to set the record straight, Mrs. Valdés poses another question: "Is 41 read as fourteen? Forty-one? Or either way? Make up your mind, and then raise your hand when I state the option you agree with. We will continue with this tomorrow."

Mrs. Valdés surveys the class, making note of the student's choices. And saves the information for her next step tomorrow. She knows that simply telling students 41 is read fourteen is not enough to completely resolve this cognitive dissonance that the students have discovered. She will revisit this discussion with some tools, models and activities fostering a shift in thinking where it is needed. One simple question (How are these the same but different?) accompanied by the right juxtaposing images to bring out naive conceptions changes understanding.

Intermediate Grades

The teaching of fractions in the intermediate grades introduces students to this new kind of numbers and a new way that numbers behave. There are many aspects about fractions that require students to rethink some of what they believed to be true about numbers. Additionally, there is a new set of words and language to be learned that apply to fractions. They are both exciting and mysterious and can be taught with sensemaking at the forefront versus a call to memorize rules.

A naive conception for students when learning about fractions is that when a shape is divided into three parts, each piece is called one-third. This early conception of fractions is incomplete and misses the critical idea that pieces need to be of equal area in order to be called thirds. By presenting students with Figure 2.8, we encourage students to build on their early understanding of how we quantify parts of one whole with fraction language.

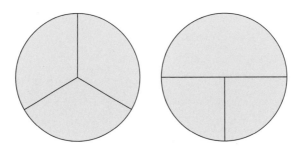

Figure 2.8

How are these the same but different?

They are the same because ....

They are the different because ....

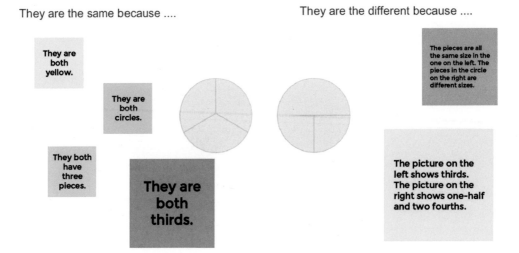

They are both yellow.

They are both circles.

They both have three pieces.

They are both thirds.

The pieces are all the same size in the one on the left. The pieces in the circle on the right are different sizes.

The picture on the left shows thirds. The picture on the right shows one-half and two fourths.

Figure 2.9

Here's how students responded to this Same But Different, shown in Figure 2.9.

Notice the pink and the yellow comment. In this example, all student responses are recorded. There is an obvious difference of opinion that has now been brought into the forefront of this classroom. Like in the kindergarten example earlier, there is disagreement and cognitive tension for some students. When this happens with students, you can almost literally see the wheels turning. Mr. Abbott takes this opportunity to turn this into a question for discussion saying, "Ryan says they are both thirds. Alex says one shows thirds and the other shows a half and two-fourths. Let's all think about this. Which answer do you agree with and why? Please turn and talk."

The class erupts into a flurry of conversation and adamant exclamations such as "They can't both show thirds. They look different."

After three minutes of talking, Mr. Abbott brings the class back together. Ryan says, "I'd like to revise my thinking. They can't both show thirds. I see what Alex is saying."

Mr. Abbott responds, "Ryan, would you come up to the board and tell us more about your thinking?"

"Sure, see in order to be thirds all of the pieces have to be equal in size. These pieces are not equal. See? This top piece is half of the circle. On the bottom, the half has been cut in half. You can imagine there being 4 of those pieces in the whole circle. So those are fourths."

Some very big ideas have just been put forth into the classroom. Mr. Abbott asks one more student to put into her own words what Ryan has just shared and ends the discussion saying, "OK. We have a lot to think about here. Let's take out our journals and write up your own answer to this: How are these two images the same but different? We will revisit this more tomorrow."

We shift students from naive conceptions to powerful understanding when we move them to see discrepancies in their thinking for themselves. *Same But Different Math* changes thinking.

> **List naive conceptions for the concepts that you teach. What images, numbers or words might you use in creating a same-but-different task for your students?**
>
> _____
>
> _____
>
> _____
>
> _____
>
> _____

Concepts Learned in Pairs

In mathematics, there are concepts that are learned in pairs. These are perfect for using the *Same But Different Math* routine, as this can help students pay attention to both the overlap and the distinguishing features.

Early Childhood

Geometry is ripe with concepts learned in pairs. A classic example is learning about rectangles and squares. Typically, these two shapes are introduced in preschool or kindergarten and are treated as two entirely different shapes. Students learn that there are squares and there are rectangles; however, squares and rectangles actually are not distinct. They overlap in definition. We can help students make sense of how squares and rectangles are both the same but different by having a conversation about this apparent contradiction – the gray space (Figure 2.10).

Figure 2.10

Here's how students responded to this *Same But Different Math* image (Figure 2.11).

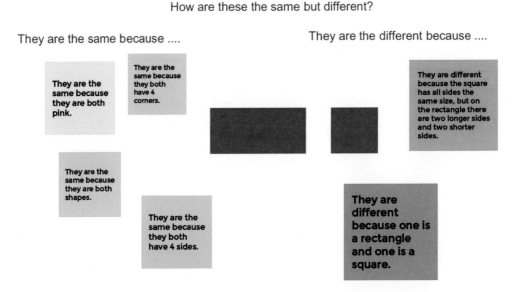

Figure 2.11

There is actually much more that is the same about these images than is different. You can see in Figure 2.11 that the students are attending to the important features of the shapes – number of sides, number of corners and length of the sides. You can also see in the differences that these students believe squares and rectangles are completely distinct shapes. They do not see that a square can be both. It is hard for students to make sense of this statement: "All squares are rectangles but not all rectangles are squares." Armed with this information, first-grade teacher Ms. Peters knows her next move. She needs to help her students untangle and yet connect these two ideas. She takes all this information in and then asks, "What is a rectangle?"

The conversation that follows allows students to land in the distinguishing features of shapes and helps students make sense of the larger category. In this case, in the hierarchy of shapes, rectangles sit at the top, with squares being a special case. Rectangles have 4 sides and 4 right angles. Squares do too, but they happen to also have equal sides.

Intermediate Grades

In addition to geometry, the study of measurement concepts is also ripe with concepts learned in pairs. One good example of this is area and perimeter (Figure 2.12). Even if these are not taught at the same time, students eventually make connections to these two concepts and are often confused. Which term means the distance around a shape, and which means the space inside of a shape? Asking students what is the same but different allows students to acknowledge this confusion and make sense of the connection between the language and the distinguishing solution path for each of these tasks.

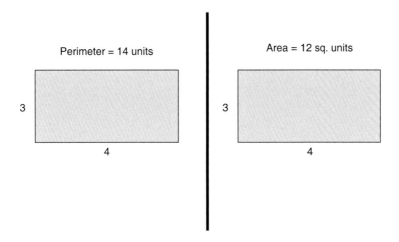

Figure 2.12

Here's how students responded to this *Same But Different Math* image (Figure 2.13).

The responses you see in Figure 2.13 come from a fourth-grade class after having experience learning about both perimeter and area. Still, many students were having trouble separating out the two concepts. By asking students what is the *Same But Different Math* and attaching the vocabulary of area and perimeter to the images and the numbers in Figure 2.13, students were able to engage in a lively conversation about the two images. As a class, they created two robust sets of descriptors of the similarities and differences. Visually, they can see and affirm that this is confusing. Separating out area and perimeter is confusing because visually you are taking in the same information but then

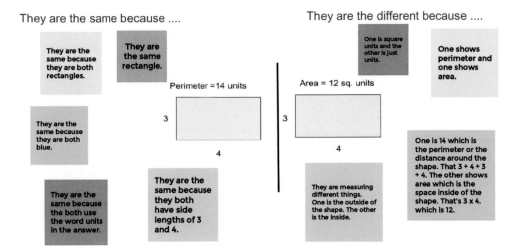

Figure 2.13

attending to a different aspect of measurement. It's inherently complex. And this is further complicated by the connection to language, much like we have seen in previous examples. Students are left with the task of which word "goes with" which concept and solution path. Sorting out which features to attend to in order to differentiate concepts that are sometimes learned in pairs, such as area and perimeter, is aided by the *Same But Different Math* routine.

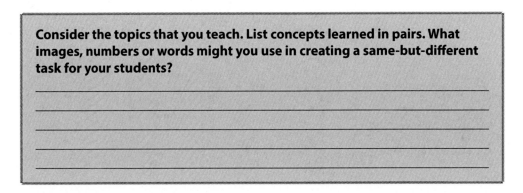

Consider the topics that you teach. List concepts learned in pairs. What images, numbers or words might you use in creating a same-but-different task for your students?

Mathematics is full of opportunities to build understanding by asking what is the same but different. You are now equipped with the tools to consider when it is best to use this routine. Sometimes you will be able to plan for this as you choose an image to build understanding, however, often you will notice something in the moment or as you engage in the Teaching for Number Sense Cycle. In doing so, you are helping students build a robust understanding of the mathematics that they are learning.

3

A Routine With Students at the Center
Part 1 of the Protocol

How can you set up the routine to provide equitable learning opportunities that encourage student agency? How do you use *Same But Different Math* to maximize student learning?

The ideas that underlie *Same But Different Math* are not only a way of both learning and growing mathematical ideas, but also they are an analogy for life. WE are all the SAME but also very different. And it is in acknowledging both that our world is enriched. *Same But Different Math* is a beautiful math routine in that it mirrors life.

Same But Different Math is set up as a routine that promotes equity – that is, all students are viewed as powerful contributors to a mathematical dialogue driving toward a shared understanding of mathematics. One voice does not dominate the conversation, nor is one correct answer the goal. Rather, the routine is set up in a way to maximize opportunities for the development of agency and a positive math identity.

Schoenfeld tells us that agency is when

students have the opportunity to generate and share ideas, both in whole class and small group settings; the extent to which student contributions are encouraged, recognized and supported as part of regular classroom activity; and the extent to which student ideas are built upon as the classroom constructs its collective understandings. People's dispositions and identities – e.g., "I am a reader," or "I'm just not a history person," – are derived from experiences with the discipline. Such dispositions and identities, often formed

DOI: 10.4324/9781003228134-4

in the classroom, shape the ways in which people relate to the discipline for the rest of their lives.

(Schoenfeld & The Teaching for
Robust Understanding Project, 2016)

Using a very intentional protocol for *Same But Different Math*, agency is fostered, and students work in a way that each student has an equal opportunity to impact the discussion. Each step in the protocol is based on well-established, intentional teaching moves.

As I unpack the protocol, in the first three steps, I focus on the student's role. In the next chapter, I unpack the last three steps and the role of the teacher.

Same But Different Math Protocol

Step 1: Look carefully at the images.

Step 2: Think silently for 1 minute.

Step 3: Turn and talk to a partner or your group.

Step 4: Share ideas as a whole class.

Step 5: Summarize ideas.

They are the same because _____. They are different because _____.

Step 6 (optional): Create one of your own.

 Looney Math

www.samebutdifferentmath.com

Figure 3.1

Same But Different Journal Page
Look carefully at the images. How are they the same but different?

Record your ideas on the chart below.

Same   Different

The are the same because
_____
_____

They are different because
_____
_____

Looney Math
www.samebutdifferentmath.com

Figure 3.1 *Continued*

Steps 1 and 2 are designed to give all students an opportunity to process the information before sharing a solution. As a class, there is no pressure – just a joyful experience in looking and thinking. These steps are critical as they are the invitation into mathematics. All are welcome.

Step 1: Look Carefully at the Image

This step cues to students that they are taking in visual information and noticing what they observe. The task of noticing and looking is less stressful than speaking and answering. The process begins there.

Step 2: Think Silently for 1 Minute

It is useful to set a timer for the full minute. This thinking time is critical. Stahl (1985) defined *think time*

> *as a distinct period of uninterrupted silence by the teacher and all students so that they both can complete appropriate information processing tasks, feelings, oral responses, and actions . . . the primary academic purpose and activity of this period of silence – to allow students and the teacher to complete on-task thinking.*

When students are given this time to think, many things happen. The pressure to produce a quick correct answer is alleviated. Students receive the message that time is required to give a thoughtful response. It is important that during this time, everyone is silently thinking. No one is raising their hands to indicate they want to speak. This is a silent period of thinking to prepare to share ideas.

Step 3: Turn and Talk to a Partner or Group

In using the turn-and-talk move, every student has an opportunity to speak and to listen. This move allows for full participation.

> *The turn-and-talk routine increases students' opportunities to respond. In traditional classrooms, the teacher asks a question and one student answers. When teachers use the turn-and-talk routine instead, all students have an opportunity to answer questions or discuss key content. Research shows that having multiple opportunities to respond and actively engage in content learning improves student learning.*
> (Stewart & Swanson, 2019)

Providing a sentence frame can support the sharing of ideas. Students share their ideas with their partner or small group by filling in the sentence frame:

They are the same because _____.
They are different because _____.

Sentence frames provide a scaffold for expressive language and give students an entry point into the conversation.

It is equally important for students to practice *thoughtful listening* as their partner is talking. This is a skill that grows with practice. One way in which to encourage thoughtful listening is to tell students that you'd like them to share something their partner said.

The focus in these first three steps is on the students and what they are doing. Let's break down all the cognitive actions that are taking place:

Thinking
Observing
Noticing
Describing
Connecting
Speaking
Summarizing

In Chapter 1, we looked at the research behind the why of *Same But Different Math* as a powerful example of compare and contrast. The protocol aligns with what Silver (2010) tells us are the Four Phases of Successful Comparison:

Description
Comparison
Conclusion
Application

In steps 1 through 3 of the protocol, students are engaged in description and comparison. They are supported with ample time for the description phase. As you saw in the examples from Chapter 2, the first comments that are typically shared pertain to what students see. This includes color and shape. That visual information is readily available, and the first pass through the comparison conversation answers the question, "What do you see?" This is the noticing phase, and students first notice what is most obvious.

Students are then engaged in comparison when they are tasked with completing the two sentences: They are the same because _____. They are different because _____. At this point, the students add in their voice, moving their thinking from strict observation and visual inspection to attaching language and a social component to their understanding. In step 3, when they turn and talk, they begin to solidify their thoughts.

In this next chapter, we turn our attention to the teacher moves in steps 4 through 6 of the protocol.

4

Teacher Moves

Part 2 of the Protocol

Now that you've had a lively conversation and provided opportunities for student agency, what do you do as the teacher to facilitate the discussion? How does the *Same But Different Math* routine conclude?

The next phase of the *Same But Different Math* protocol involves the teacher's moves and decisions now that the students' thinking has been made public. Building on the Four Phases of Successful Comparison (Silver, 2010), we now work with conclusion and application.

Step 4: Share Ideas as a Whole Class

This is the step in which students come back together as a full class and share their thinking. By coming together and gathering ideas in writing, shared meaning is created as a community of thinkers.

Psychologist Lev Vygotsky in 1962 examined how social environments influence the learning process concluding that we learn through our interactions and communications with others. He suggested that learning takes place through the interactions students have with their peers, teachers and other experts.

Building on this, the protocol involves students sharing their ideas as a whole class.

The teacher's role is then to provide a forum for the social context for learning through the sharing of ideas.

DOI: 10.4324/9781003228134-5

How is this done equitably?

I am definitely dating myself, but I am probably not alone in remembering the iconic hand raising and shouting out of Arnold Horshack from the 1970s' sitcom *Welcome Back Kotter* (worth googling for a laugh!) Here we have a room full of disengaged students except for Horshack, who is jumping out of his skin and shouting, "Oh, Oh, Oh!" in order to be called on.

When asking students to share, some students will then raise their hands, and others will not. The teacher now has an on-the-spot decision to make. Whom should they call on? What if only some students raised their hands? What if no students raised their hands? Posing a question and asking for hands up for a correct response places the teacher in a position to make multiple in-the-moment decisions.

With a call for sharing and hands raised, ultimately, the teacher has to call on one student to answer what was asked. In this type of interaction, two people are participating – the teacher and the student called on. The rest of the class may or may not be listening. The student selected for that moment in time holds significant status in the classroom. They are the person being validated. For the rest of the students, they are observers in this interaction. Often with this practice, over time, certain students grow to be perceived as the experts in the room. These are the students whom a teacher may rely on as "go to" students to call on when they are hoping someone will provide a particular insight. Teachers know who these students are, as do the rest of the students in the classroom. If the goal of asking a question is to provide an opportunity for everyone to learn from what is being asked, this process is problematic as this creates issues with access and equity.

When only one person is chosen to respond to a question, the learning opportunities for the other students in the room are compromised.

Carrie Cole (2017) of Side by Side Consulting warns that

> *the overused classroom practice of hand-raising contributes significantly to the achievement gap in our schools. Essentially, when we tell students to raise their hands to answer, we are sending the message that they can choose whether they want to participate in the lesson. Further, of those students who are raising their hands, only 25% are participating consistently. Additionally, when we think about the students who often raise their hands the most – who are they? Clearly, they are the students who most often know the answers.*

Now, let's think about this from the perspective of *Same But Different Math*. After students have had time to think, share, and formulate an answer, it is important to gather the ideas from around the room. One way to share is to have every student write their idea on a whiteboard and then the teacher scans the room looking for common solutions. This strategy allows the teacher to assess how each and every student has chosen to answer the question.

Another strategy for sharing ideas is to ask for three volunteers. While hands may be raised at this point, this is not cold calling as everyone has had an opportunity to think, talk, listen, and maybe even write about their solution during the turn and talk. This final stage is simply a gathering of ideas versus fishing for correct answers.

Which three students will share their ideas is determined by the teacher who has walked around listening to the turn and talk that just took place. You strategically choose who will share and the order in which they will share, allowing for multiple perspectives, including answers that are both correct and incorrect. It is critical to hear a variety of voices as you create an equitable community of learners through the *Same But Different Math* routine.

As students are sharing ideas, the teacher is recording them – writing them down and organizing thoughts as they are shared. As students share, categorize their ideas by asking – is this a way they are the same or that they are different? It is useful to use a graphic organizer to help students make sense of the information that is collectively shared.

Step 5: Summarize

During this step, the teacher summarizes the student's ideas, clarifying the key outcomes of the discussion. It is at this point that you restate the students' ideas and the concepts discussed, calling attention to the important mathematics from the discussion. You've selected the image for a particular mathematical reason in mind; this step is critical to concretize the concepts that are shared in the whole-group discussion.

It is helpful to summarize the group share by using the same sentence stems from the turn and talk: They are the same because _____. They are different because _____. How would you summarize the *Same But Different Math* talk that follows (Figure 4.1)?

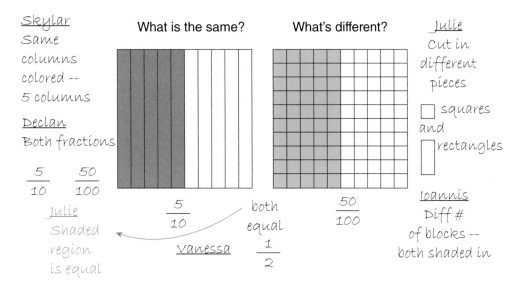

Figure 4.1

They are the same because:

_____
_____

They are different because:

_____
_____

Summarizing forces the conversation to go back to purpose. Why have you selected this image (Figure 4.1) to have a mathematical conversation? What learning are you hoping for? Your purpose now is to integrate what has been put forth by the students. They may or may not have arrived at the place of understanding you anticipated, but it is your job to tie things together.

You might summarize Figure 4.1 like this.

The two images are the same because, as Julia said, they both show the same amount of area shaded in. And Vanessa reminded us that in both cases they are showing 1/2. They are different, however, because like Ioannis shared, both pictures have a different number of pieces shaded in, and Julie shared that those pieces are different. So we can have the same fractional amount of a rectangle shaded in, but that space can be divided differently.

This step is in line with Silver's step of conclusion for comparisons. This is the step in which you "discuss what you have learned from your comparison" (Silver, 2010). And, as a teacher, it is your job to articulate that clearly for your students.

Step 6: Create One of Our Own (Optional)

The final step is the opportunity for students to create their own same but different that exemplifies or builds on the one that was just discussed. In doing so, students are working on the last phase of comparison, which is application. Here you have the opportunity to see if students have processed the information and made sense of it in a way that they can create another example.

Please note that this moves the routine from an activity to a full lesson. It takes time for students to synthesize all that they've learned and make their own creations. Time is necessary for students to demonstrate that they own the concept and are able to take this next step.

Recommendations for this step are as follows:

1. Use only with certain images when you want to assess more closely for understanding.
2. Allow this as an optional choice for students who want to go further – that is, assign for choice time or as homework.

To support this work, start slowly. For example, if students are struggling to get started, you can give students one image and ask them to create the second contrasting image. In this way, the opportunity to create is there, but it is structured in a supportive way. Other students will appreciate the creativity and open-endedness of creating one entirely of their own.

Building on the earlier example, you might give students the image in Figure 4.2 and ask them to create a comparative image.

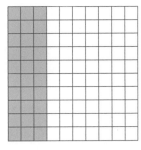

Figure 4.2

When students do take the time to create their own *Same But Different Math*, it is important that they are able to share their work and listen to conversations about their image. You may allow for a gallery walk for students to see one another's examples. Or you may allow for students to conduct their own *Same But Different Math* lesson with a partner, small group or even with the whole class.

As you've seen, each one of the six steps as described is intentionally designed and based on best practice. The *Same But Different Math* protocol has been created to maximize the opportunities for learning.

5

Now It's Your Turn!

You are now well versed in all aspects of the *Same But Different Math* number sense routine. Let's review some key ideas from each chapter and talk about planning. Rather than me taking away your opportunities to solidify your learning and providing those summaries, I'm going to prompt you with some questions for you to summarize the first four chapters.

Review and Summary of Your Learning

Chapter 1: Why Should I Use This Routine?
In Chapter 1, we explored the research behind the power of the routine.

> **What is grayscale thinking, and how does that come into play with this routine?**
> _____
> _____
> _____
> _____

DOI: 10.4324/9781003228134-6

> **Why is Same But Different a powerful math routine? What does the research tell us?**
>
> _____
> _____
> _____
> _____

Chapter 2: When Should I Use This Routine?

In Chapter 2, we explored how you can choose and select images that connect to your students' needs.

> **What are the three cases in which you have an opportunity to use Same But Different Math?**
>
> _____
> _____
> _____
> _____

Chapters 3 and 4: How Do I Use This Routine?

In Chapters 3 and 4, you learned the protocol for using the *Same But Different Math*. The way in which this routine plays out is critical in creating equitable learning experiences, allowing students to have autonomy and authority over their learning.

> **In what ways does the Same But Different math support equity in the classroom?**
>
> _____
> _____
> _____
> _____

> **What are the 6 steps of the Same But Different protocol, and why is each step important?**
>
> _____
> _____
> _____
> _____

Now That You've Taken Some Time to Revisit, Review and Summarize Your Learning, Let's Turn Our Attention to Putting This Into Action Planning

As you learned throughout the book, opportunities will come up naturally to ask what is the same but different throughout your instruction. I'd like to talk about how you plan for this. At the beginning of a unit of instruction, you can take a moment and plan to use this routine intentionally. Here's what that would look like.

As you prepare to begin a unit of study, you are unpacking the standards for the topic at hand. What do you want students to understand as a result of this unit? What are the key ideas and standards? While you are doing this, think about the three cases of when to use *Same But Different Math* from Chapter 2:

1. Connecting concepts
2. Naive conceptions
3. Concepts learned in pairs

You can use the following templates to plan for each of these cases within the upcoming unit of study.

Connecting concepts

What is the current standard? What do you want your students to learn as a result of this unit of study?	What did your students learn last year about this topic? What is their foundation for this work?
Match with two images.	

As you look further into the goals of the unit, are there any concepts that are going to be taught in pairs? Can you create or find a *Same But Different Math* image to help your students make sense of those ideas?

Naive conceptions

What are some common naive conceptions you anticipate will come up in this unit?	What is the concept you wish for your students to understand?
Match with an image for each.	

Concepts learned in pairs

Identify concepts from the unit that might be confused with one another.	
Match with an image for each concept.	

In addition to knowing why, when and how to use the routine and creating your own images, images by topic can be found at www.samebutdifferentmath.com (Figure 5.1). Here you will find a range of images for you to consider for use in your classroom.

SAME BUT DIFFERENT MATH from 🅜 Looney Math

Developing Grayscale Thinking

ABOUT   ADDITION/SUBTRACTION   EARLY NUMERACY   MULTIPLICATION/DIVISION   MEASUREMENT   PLACE VALUE   FRACTIONS, RATIOS, ETC   GEOMETRY   ALGEBRA

Figure 5.1

You can choose an image from the website and plan for the *Same But Different Math* lesson. You can do so thoughtfully using the following template.

Same But Different Math Planning Guide	
What concept are you looking to explore? Why?	
Which image are you selecting? Why?	
What do you anticipate students will say is the **same** about these images?	
What do you anticipate students will say is **different** about these images?	
What vocabulary might come up in the discussion?	
What naive conceptions might students hold about the concept?	
Given what you anticipate, write a summarizing statement of what you anticipate happening as a conclusion to the lesson.	
Other notes:	

Visit the website now (www.samebutdifferentmath.com) and practice using the template.

Here is an example of one that has been filled in for you.

Same But Different Math Planning Guide	
What concept are you looking to explore? Why?	Using a known fact to determine a new fact. I am working on building fact fluency with my students. They know their doubles pretty well. I am hoping to explore the idea of doubles plus 1.

Same But Different Math Planning Guide	
Which image are you selecting?	I am choosing this image because I am going to be introducing the strategy of doubles plus 1 OR the idea of using a known fact to determine an unknown fact.
What do you anticipate students will say is the **same** about these images?	They are the same because they both show frogs. They both have yellow and red. They are both arranged in pairs. They both have 12 frogs in them.
What do you anticipate students will say is **different** between these images?	They are different because one has an extra frog. There is one more yellow frog that isn't in a pair. One is 12 and one is 13.
What vocabulary might come up in the discussion?	Pair, doubles, addition, rows, columns, even, odd
What naive conceptions might students hold about the concept?	I might see students counting all and not applying fact knowledge. Students might not notice the connection of the second image being one more than the first one or that the first image shows 6 + 6.
Given what you anticipate, write a summarizing statement of what you anticipate happening as a conclusion to the lesson.	They are the same because they both show frogs, and we can find out how many bears by using addition. They are different because the first picture shows 6 + 6 and the second picture shows 6 + 7. And 6 + 7 has one more bear. 6 + 6 = 12 and 6 + 7 = 13, which is just one more.
Other notes:	Students might not see the addition facts of 6 + 6 and 6 + 7. They might focus on things grouped in twos and counting by twos. They might not make the connection between the two images. If this happens, I will try using a different image showing doubles and then doubles plus 1 on a tens frame.

Conclusion

You have read research, examples, tasks and questions. You've looked deeply at the why, when and how of the routine. If I've done my job, you are energized and ready to go. How will your students feel about this routine? This comment sums it all up quite well:

> *Same but different is awesome! Whenever we do this in math, I'm always having little explosions of understanding and connections happening in my brain. It's like, OH – I never thought about that before, but now that makes sense!*
>
> (Sonya, Grade 4)

You are now equipped with a robust understanding of the *Same But Different Math* routine. You can bring bursts of sensemaking and joy to your students in powerful ways. You are able to teach your students a way of thinking about math and beyond as they make sense of all new learning.

Thank you for taking this journey with me.

References

Chapter 1

From Harvard University Center for the Developing Child. Retrieved from https://developingchild.harvard.edu/.

Marzano, R., Pickering, D., & Pollock, J. (2010). *Classroom instruction that works: Research-based strategies for increasing student achievement* (1st ed.). Alexandria, VA: ASCD.

Meltzer, L. (2007). *Executive functioning education: From theory to practice.* New York: Guilford Press.

Silver, H. (2010). *Compare & contrast: Teaching comparative thinking to strengthen student learning.* Alexandria, VA: ASCD.

Van de Walle, J. A. (2013). *Elementary and middle school mathematics: Teaching developmentally.* Boston: Pearson.

Williams, B. (2006). *Black and White thinking doesn't work in a gray world.* Retrieved from www.eastbaytimes.com/2006/09/30/black-and-white-thinking-doesnt-work-in-a-gray-world/

Chapter 2

Fujii, T. (2014). Misconceptions and alternative conceptions in mathematics education. In S. Lerman (Ed.), *Encyclopedia of mathematics education.* Dordrecht: Springer. https://doi.org/10.1007/978-94-007-4978-8_114

Sullivan, P., & Mousley, J. (2001). Thinking teaching: Seeing mathematics teachers as active decision makers. In F. L. Lin & T. J. Cooney (Eds.), *Making sense of mathematics teacher education.* Dordrecht: Springer. https://doi.org/10.1007/978-94-010-0828-0_7

Chapter 3

Schoenfeld, A. H., & The Teaching for Robust Understanding Project. (2016). *An introduction to the teaching for robust understanding (TRU) framework.* Berkeley, CA: Graduate School of Education. Retrieved from http://truframework.org or http://map.mathshell.org/trumath.php

Silver, H. F. (2010). *Compare & contrast: Teaching comparative thinking to strengthen student learning.* Alexandria, VA: ASCD.

(Stahl 1985). "Think-Time" and "Wait-Time" Skillfully in the Classroom retrieved from https://files.eric.ed.gov/fulltext/ED370885.pdf

Stewart, A. A., & Swanson, E. (2019). *Turn and talk: An evidence-based practice. Teacher's guide.* Austin, TX: The Meadows Center for Preventing Educational Risk. Retrieved from www.meadowscenter.org/files/resources/TurnAndTalk_TeacherGuide.pdf

Chapter 4

Cole, C. (2017). *No raised hands: The 5 step questioning method.* Retrieved from www.google.com/url?q=http://sidebysideconsulting.com/2017/09/18/no-raised-hands-the-5-step-questioning-method/&sa=D&source=editors&ust=1631297437850000&usg=AOvVaw1dLP4U4sR1XPzHVm-OBUNg

Silver, H. (2010). *Compare & contrast: Teaching comparative thinking to strengthen student learning.* Alexandria, VA: ASCD.

Vygotsky, L. S. (1962). *Thought and language.* Cambridge, MA: MIT Press (Original work published in 1934).

Appendix A: Poem

Same But Different

The stars below are the same. You can see.
Let's count them together. 1, 2, 3!

They are different as well.
Look again. Can you tell?

The stars on one side are lined up in a row.
The stars on the other? Well, in a triangle they go!

They are the same but different. How can that be?
Not one or the other? Come explore more with me!

Look at each picture. How are they the same?
Then see how they are different – that is my game!

Appendix B: Additional Images

They are the same because . . .

They are different because . . .

They are the same because . . .

They are different because . . .

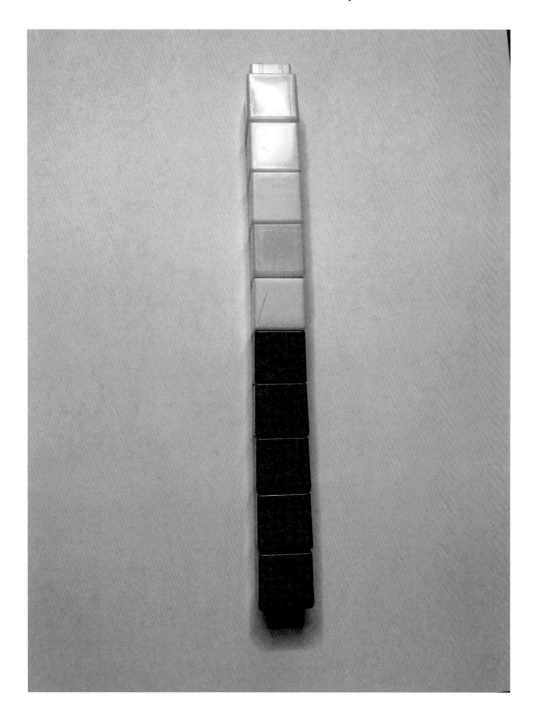

They are the same because . . .

They are different because . . .

They are the same because . . .

They are different because . . .

They are the same because . . .

They are different because . . .

They are the same because . . .

They are different because . . .

They are the same because . . .

They are different because . . .

They are the same because . . .

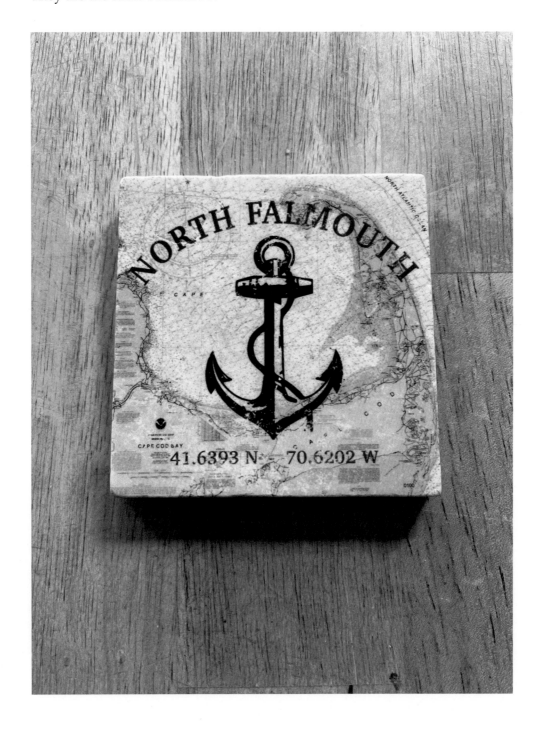

They are different because . . .

They are the same because . . .

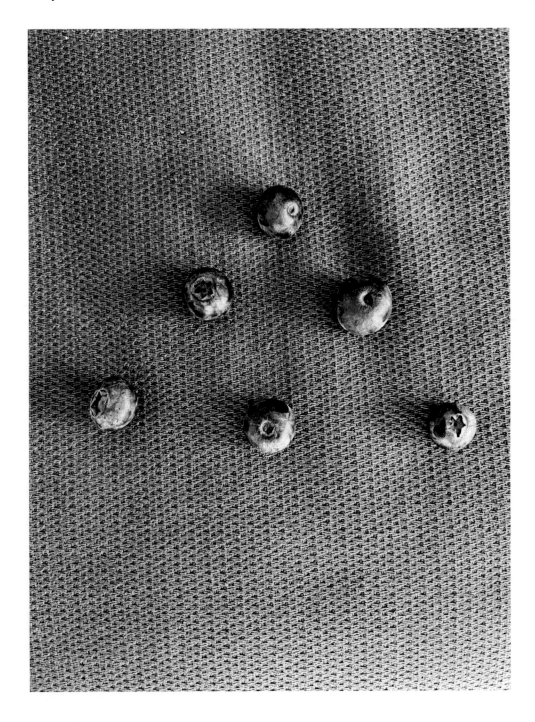

They are different because . . .

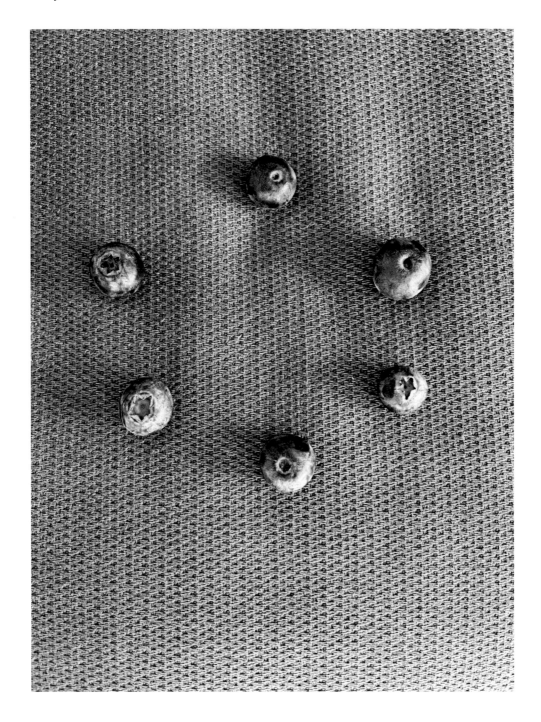

They are the same because . . .

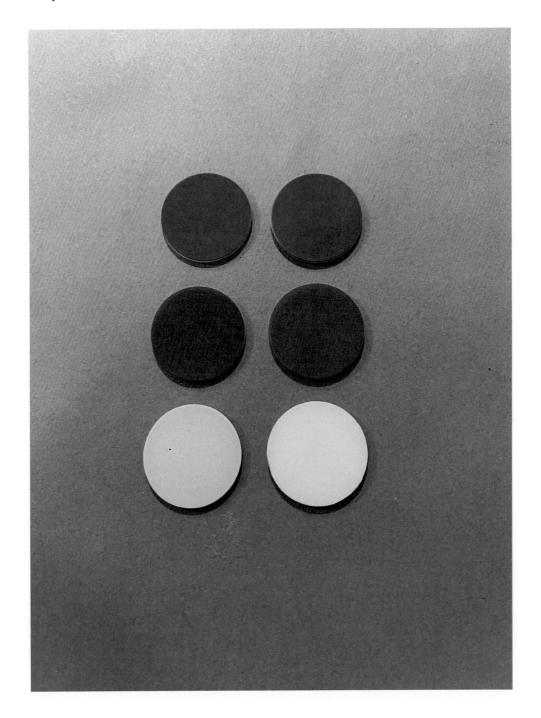

They are different because . . .

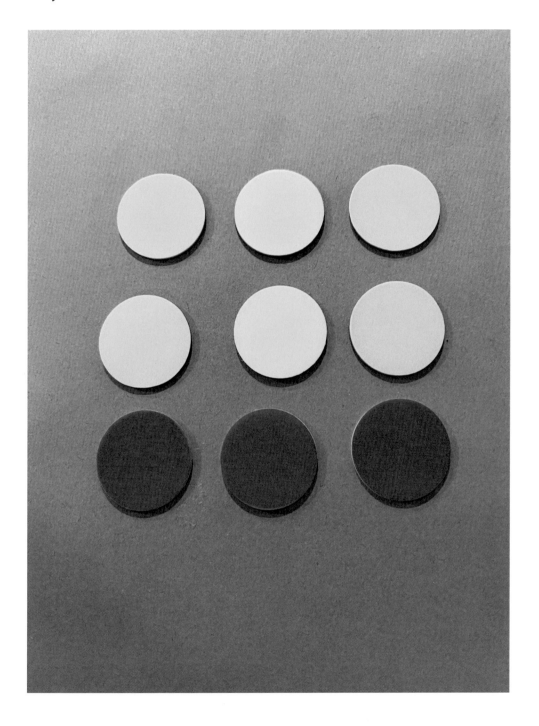

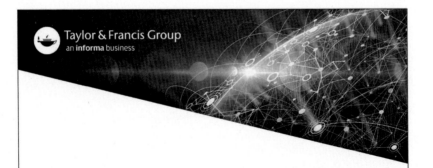